The Musician's Book of Five Rings

**Samurai Strategies of Miyamoto Musashi
For Excellence and Ascension of Performance**

Stephen F. Kaufman, Hanshi

Published by Jamey Aebersold Jazz
PO Box 1244
New Albany, IN 47150
staff@jazzbooks.com

ISBN 978-1-56224-323-4

Kaufman, Stephen F., 1939 -

Musician's Book of Five Rings (The) –
Samurai Strategies of Miyamoto Musashi
for Excellence and Ascension of Performance

1. Book of Five Rings, 2. Miyamoto Musashi, 3. Musicianship,
4. Strategy, 5. Performance

Book design by Stephen F. Kaufman

Author photos – Shmuel Biopcik
Author headshot – Peggy A Thompson

1 3 5 7 9 2 4 6 8 10

for

Joe Allard, Maestro

My teacher, who I never truly appreciated

and

Sidney Shanman, Drummer

My uncle, who laid a Charlie Parker 78 on me

when I was but 12

Contents

INTRODUCTION

You are holding in your hands a most unusual book. A true, modern-day samurai, a master practitioner of the art of the sword, has adapted the centuries-old principles of attaining excellence in the martial arts to show you how to become a master in the field of music. This book is a roadmap into the mastery process—it will outline the process, step-by-step, toward the dual goal of self-mastery and mastery of the art of musicianship and performance.

Drawing on the work of the legendary Japanese martial artist Miyamoto Musashi, you will learn, among many other things, the most effective way to develop the discipline needed to be a great musician, the way to approach a musical performance, the importance of tradition in developing your art, and, most importantly, the over-arching ATTITUDE of mastery that will empower you to reach your highest musical potential.

In this day and age, it is most rare to find an individual that has devoted his life to this process of dual mastery—over oneself and one's art. Hanshi Steve Kaufman is the real deal! He lives what he teaches and continues to dedicate his life to refining the highest principles of discipline and performance within himself and to share his extensive wisdom with countless aspiring students worldwide.

If you dream of being a great musician, the principles outlined in this book can light your path so that you, a realized master of your art, can burst forth into the world as a blazing artistic fire!

Dave Frank
Author, Joy of Improv, Vol. 1+2 (Hal Leonard)
Assoc. Prof. of Piano, Berklee College of Music
Director, Dave Frank School of Jazz, NYC

PREFACE

Miyamoto Musashi considered the greatest swordsman Japan has ever produced is revered as the "sword saint" because of his historical importance and legendary exploits. The original intention of his masterpiece, *The Book of Five Rings*, was to offer firm advice for warriors involved with mortal combat: the motivation to win and survive. However, when looked at relative to personal endeavor, the principles of his philosophy are universally important for the empowerment and personal mastery of an individual, regardless of any discipline.

As author of the world's best-known interpretation of Musashi's *Book of Five Rings* and having practiced martial arts for many years, and as a performing musician, a saxophonist (still active in both disciplines), I have taken it upon myself to explain in fervent detail the knowledge required to succeed in the endeavors of budding artists, students, and professional musicians.

The principles of swordsmanship and execution of perfection of one's chosen craft are the same, with no variation except, that in combat, a warrior takes lives, but the exquisite performance of music can abduct a soul and elevate a listener to heights of splendid joy when performed by a musician, with oneness of endeavor and a developed sense of self.

The sword master and the master musician incorporate a like commitment to perfection in the arena of life. It is the purposeful application of the qualities and the "spirit of the thing itself" that is the difference between life and death when wielding a sword or playing perfect notes and creating life through music.

In this book, you will learn the wisdom needed to control your own universe. The lessons I teach are in the voice of Miyamoto Musashi, as he would speak directly to you. He is stern at times and gruff, seemingly without mercy, yet you will find great compassion in his words as I interpret them for you, musician to musician. You will find many repetitions to his words, and there is good purpose for this approach, as you will come to understand. Think in terms of theme and variation.

My intention is to guide you toward becoming the greatest musician that ever lived. How you interpret these words is your own personal matter. Certainly, constant practice is a requirement for ascension in any form of expression, and that is a given. The profound and timeless revelations of Musashi have lasted for more than 350 years and can empower you to catapult to the greatness you seek. I constantly stress practice in all forms of growth and development throughout the book as it applies to the realization of your dreams and goals as a profound and exceptionally creative musician.

Stephen F. Kaufman,
New York, 2018
www.hanshi.com

The Master Greets You

My name is Miyamoto Musashi. I have beaten over sixty battle-tested warriors in personal combat and duels. As I approached my sixtieth year, I took a step back, and, reflecting upon my life, and, in a flash of insight and wisdom, came to understand my great success. Having been virtuous and especially gifted was something that never fazed me as to my abilities, in as much as the probable reason for it to have manifested in my life. Regardless of the thoughts of others, the good or bad aspects of their study and training, even possibly simple good luck, may or may not have had anything to do with it. What I believe was the main reason for my personal growth and ascension was simply that I willed it, demanded it for myself, and constantly studied and practiced from dawn to dusk, even into the night. I had only one thing in my mind, and that was to become the consummate practitioner of my art.

In this little book I am going to teach you the why and wherefore of *all* profound accomplishment. At times, you will think that I am simply repeating myself, over and again, and it is good that you recognize that. It is for the express purpose of enforcing my teachings upon you until they are part of your psyche and become irrefutable. By constant repetition, you will learn the reality of my strategy, and I will not leave it to you to grasp my meanings in a superficial manner.

I give you *The Book of Five Rings* in five sections called Earth, Water, Fire, Wind, and No-thing. The fundamental basis of my teaching is in the book of Earth, which lays the foundation and groundwork for the entire, practical philosophy of strategy. Water explains the natural flow of things; Fire, the passion for accomplishment; Wind, the ambiguities of meaningless presumption and, finally, the way of No-thing-ness as the true nature of being.

The Book of Earth represents the foundation and the groundwork of any art or craft and introduces you to a complete familiarization with the fundamentals as well as why it is essential to understand the mechanisms of other arts and disciplines. It is difficult to understand the universe by only acknowledging the sun and the moon; there are countless aspects, including stars, comets, and planets along with countless other galaxies and universe. Endeavor to know everything you can about any particular environment in which you include yourself. Though this may seem daunting at first, the reality is that once you are aware of other aspects in *your* universe, other universes will reveal the same truths, though with a different perspective. To know about these things will assist you in becoming more proficient in your own understanding and empower you to become excellent in your self-presentation as well as giving you additional tools to perform on higher levels of consciousness and musicianship. Contemplation of these matters is essential if you are to ascend to the magnificence of your desires and dreams.

The Book of Water explains how all things flow with a natural rhythm in appropriate space and time. Water fills all shapes regardless of other impositions as to its functionality. All things are eventually worn away by water—*all* things— and so you should think in terms of being able to wear away any impediments to your life and artistic development by not considering any form of impossibility or submitting to unreasonable fears that you may or may not self-impose. With correct determination, you will conquer any difficulty that presents itself, regardless of the form it represents. It is your consciousness that determines how you will ascend to mastery, and no amount of coercion from any source, positive or negative, will empower you to do this without your ardent desire to do it for yourself and for the art you practice. Reality is mostly intuitive, and the more you apply yourself to the acceptance of your own greatness, your greatness will empower itself in you, as you, and through you in all aspects of your life experiences.

The Book of Fire is about passion: your intentions and the manner in which you provide your soul with exultation and joy. Total commitment to your work will give you a thrill of accomplishment that impels you to further your expressions of self through your music and the music through yourself. When you practice, it must be with the intensity of the practice performance being the very last one you will ever do and the one *you* want as a remembrance, not for others to remember you, but for your own sense of being and self-worth. Keep in mind that you are the center of the universe, and you have this incredible gift to share with the rest of the world; you must not squander it with insecurities. When you perform with passion and fire, the joy and thrill of doing so will illuminate your passion even further, empowering you to perform on a more convincing and inspired level each time you practice. When practicing, know you are performing for the largest audience in the world, and your actions will radiate through the exquisite giving of your music in you, as you, and through you. There is no other way.

In the *Book of Wind*, I tell you about the follies and fantasies of yourself and others who merely want recognition for themselves and not for their devotion to any aspect of their life, including their chosen discipline or art. This is a terrible place to be, and you must be very conscious to avoid becoming enamored of yourself. Beware the deadliness of arrogance, conceit, and false pride. To become ensnared with these debilitating aspects of personality will cause you harm and frustration and will cause the "spirit of the thing itself" of your art to be impeded by your childish whining. Wanting to take, and take without truly giving all you have back to the Creative Power of the Universe that enlightens you personally, and not to perform for "Its" amusement and joy, will be your downfall. Be warned! You are merely the tool of the divine essence of the universe that has given you a profound gift and that you have accepted as yours: music as a tool for your soul's expression. The fanciful flights of other performers may in fact be their way to ascend to greatness, but that should not be your "way" unless you seriously identify with the external force they use to create their universe. Should you find that you are sincerely attracted to and want to perform on that level—fine, as long as you understand that you must still act with passion and not merely imitate. In order to innovate and to create new substance, it is required that you fully understand the masters that preceded you and that they must be used as the basis for evolvement; otherwise, everything becomes random nonsense for entertainment and without substance.

The *Book of No-thing* is straightforward. The first four sections are the essence of the *Book of Five Rings*. All of the above is required if you are to elevate your consciousness to a point of ultimate expression. I refer to this profound reality as No-thing. There is a "way" of nature that coincides with all that comes to pass, what is now happening and, speculatively, what will happen in the future. Understand intuitively that it is all one thing, and that this oneness is total and complete without having to refer to anything, it exists according to its own unexplainable creativity. As you will learn later, *if you know things you know, then you also know things you do not know.*

Though I have never had the benefit of a teacher, I have attained an incredible sense of self. Perhaps I am most fortunate to have had an instinct for my own personal perfection and had as a guide an internal knowingness of how to attain my goals. I have used the "spirit of the thing itself," or, perhaps, the "spirit of the thing itself" has used me. It is irrelevant. What *is* relevant is that I have attained what I wanted to attain, and I am here to teach you the very same strategy.

Read with understanding and retention. If there is something you do not comprehend at first, reread the section until you do understand. There are no mysteries in my teachings. What I am telling you is real.

And so, we begin ...

EARTH

ONE
THE BOOK OF EARTH
FOUNDATIONS

That no one is perfect is a misconception. We are all perfect in exactly the form we represent to ourselves and to the world. The idea that perfection is unattainable makes no sense. It is attainable when you believe it is. What we determine for ourselves as something that may be missing in our lives can easily be rectified and made to be perfect exactly as we see it. It is the misunderstanding of and our lack of acceptance of our own greatness that prohibits us from ascending to the ultimate position of true mastery—*our* mastery, not his, hers, or theirs. It takes great courage to stand alone at the top of the mountain; yet, it is exactly where you should want to be when you practice and dream of magnificent performance and creativity. For many, this is a new way of thinking.

If you fancy yourself a greater composer than any who have gone before you, or a more profound performer than another, then you are deluding yourself. That is not what strategy is about, and you are missing the point. Given it is essential to stand on the shoulders of the giants that preceded you, and as that particular artist is the ideal of your supposed emulation, then it is required you study everything there is to study about what that artist contributed. You can then evolve the particular mode of expression from that point, not as an imitator, but as a creator. You cannot be another person, but you can be an extension of the "spirit of the thing itself," the same spirit great artists had accepted into their psyche, consciously or not.

Once you plan your desire in your mind and heart to manifest, it should not matter to you if you do or do not ascend to preconceived ideas about your goals. Worrying about if you will or won't, can put you in a frame of mind that produces a fear of failure, the most horrific of sensibilities. However, once determination has taken root in your inner being, generally nothing can deter you from attaining your desire. The "spirit of the thing itself" will always deliver exactly what you ask for and demand. If your desire is to be the very best and to be it without question, all you need is to focus on the result and not concern yourself with smelling the flowers along the way. You will begin to do that automatically, and there will be plenty of time to do that, once you have arrived at your destination and continue to expand your horizon.

The virtue of true strategy is to strengthen your resolve while ascending to become one with the ultimate source of all reality as defined by your own self. In my world, the development of an enlightened consciousness is an ongoing thing; each experience continually leads to ever-increasing awareness of the self as I acknowledge and overcome new challenges. You can only understand the "way" by maintaining your personal integrity and maintaining determination and focus on your ideal. You cannot learn the true "way" through frivolous contests to see who can win a bigger trophy or accolade.

The True Nature of Strategy

More than likely, masters in your own world have taught you the manner in which you are to attain enlightenment relative to your chosen discipline. They have shown you the methods of the ancient masters and have told you to study them without let up and to continue studying them, even though you may think you have attained a grasp of what they talked about and how they performed. There is a very good reason that some of the ancients are thought of as masters. It is because they have influenced all those that came after them by first influencing themselves. The wise are wise because they learned and came to understand the wisdom of their predecessors in all areas of their intellect and soul. Using that wisdom, they evolved and became aware of many things and the variations attached. You as well should learn the importance of studying arts other than the music you are professing as your life's work. You play the harp and you study other stringed instruments; you study flutes and horns, then percussion and voice and other cultural instruments; the list is endless. Though these are all music-based, you must also become aware of other art forms and disciplines: painting, sewing, carpentry, basic business principles, mathematics, mechanics, and technology. This can seem daunting, and you will choose which ones intrigue you, using every means available to you for the development of your divine and earthly right to live in joy and freedom while constantly focusing on your ideal.

To become well rounded, it is necessary to see other forms of discipline and, yes, adopt some of the principles into your own craft. Why? Because you will eventually notice all things are the same except for specific characteristics.

Music, though, is something that has absolutely no functional or practical value except for expression of the soul, and that is what separates it from every other art form, without reservation. Because of music's intrinsic reality, it takes both performer and listener to a completely different dimension that is not easy to explain. To communicate with another without words or physical actions is an expression of your soul.

Comparing the Strategies of Other Arts

An artist cannot see the worth or value in his or her art without being aware of the artistry found in another discipline. Once you understand the goal of an art, it becomes relatively easy to grasp the "spirit of the thing itself." To understand economics, I study the correlation of profits, losses, debits, and assets, and so I can compare the way of the musician to the way of the accountant. To study the sword, study war, weapons, and warriors; to study artisanship, study the project, the tools, and the people employed. You may succeed or fail, depending on your attitude towards the "spirit of the thing itself," and it is irrelevant at that point as you continue to push yourself to higher levels of accomplishment. You must never let up in your study, regardless of the path you choose. As you attain higher levels of understanding and performance, it is essential to reinforce your focus with more discipline, and though you may have mastered a particular level, you must constantly search for more understanding of your chosen art. You cannot understand everything; however, once you understand *that*—you will.

Discipline

If there is no discipline, how can there be a true realization of an ideal? How can a person be trusted to perform in society if there is no understanding of what society needs, what mastery of an art requires? To act in harmony with the environment of where you are, you must observe, understand, and practice with certain rules and their inherent needs. If you do not, then you will be unable to work in harmony with other people and devices. If you cannot work in harmony, how can you expect to attain perfection in your own ideal? How can you expect to ascend to new levels of being and musical innovation if you are not aware of current trends and past developments leading to what is presently acceptable or not? It is essential to know the rules of the game: which rules work, which rules do not work, and which rules can be changed to suit a particular need and, of changed rules, which will create additional problems and those that will not.

Never Assume False Perfection

Artisans are familiar with the quality of the materials they use for certain aspects of their work. A person must not assume another person's education or instrument is an indication of his or her strength. In my world, many warriors have always relied on the "look" of their armor to intimidate the enemy and have miserably failed in their quest for winning. Do not assume that what appears as finely crafted goods will hold up under the test of usage. The truth is that strength lies in the interior of the warrior: in his heart, his mind, and his spirit. That being so, should the most elegant weapon not be available at the moment, the true master—the true warrior—uses what is at hand to create the masterpieces of his or her life. An excellently crafted instrument is incapable of acting of its own accord—it needs the heart and soul of a player to bring out its perfection. The artisan must understand the materials used for the project: strengths and weaknesses. Likewise, to produce a fine sword, a master artisan must approach his art with devotion. It is the same with instruments. In the same way, a merchant relies on his ability for getting people to believe his or her goods are the best; that is the way of the merchant. The farmer knows when his produce is good and when it is inferior; that is the way of the farmer. The hardened warrior knows in his heart when action is correct, or it is false bravado. All people are the same except for the belief in their own selves. These are their "ways," regardless of popular opinion for or against themselves. The musician, the true artist, knows when the performance given is excellent, mediocre, or, even worse, without feeling, or in the true sense of the warrior—giving.

The orchestra manager must assign positions according to the known abilities of the musicians selected for inclusion in the unit in the same manner as a supervisor on a construction job assigns tasks to his people according to their known abilities. Who is good at what specific aspect of the project? Who can lay floors, who can double on another instrument? This is true for all things when seeking perfection. The conductor must understand their personal motives before understanding the reality of leading others; it is especially true when the teaching process is involved. Only when the conductor observes and listens to each musician can the conductor know which musician will be able to perform a specific piece of music; otherwise, chaos will be the result.

The leader must circulate among the players to appraise their strengths and weaknesses and must praise when praise and admonish equally when necessary. If not, there will be a loss of morale and the performance will suffer accordingly. If this is not done with due consciousness, the leader will not know when and where to assign roles. This is a virtue of strategy. Why ask a flutist to join the string section? Even with tremendous spirit on the part of the flutist, the player's best efforts would not be on a par with that of a principle flutist.

A Musician's Responsibilities

Musicians are responsible for their own instruments as craftspeople are responsible for their own tools. It is not possible to get good results without the necessary respect for one's tools as an artist or otherwise. There must be time in training, practice, and maintenance, regardless of how gifted an artist may be. Each aspect of the craft, every aspect of the score being performed, and every aspect of the technical requirements of the instrument being played must be examined repeatedly without regard for energy and effort, either physically or mentally. The "spirit of the thing itself" is what guides a person to greatness. There is no one way to approach and petition anything for immediate ingratiation without having done the proper groundwork. The universe does not work that way. How could it and, at the same time, expect its own perfection to develop? If you permit the "spirit of the thing itself" of your music to permeate your being, the spirit will express itself through you, by permitting you to be its instrument, and your performance will be spectacular. Over time, you will come to understand the true nature of your music, and you will be self-assured as an artist. You may have heard the Samurai expression that "the sword is the soul of the samurai," but truth be told that only happens when the samurai is the soul of the sword. It is the same with an artist, and when the melding is complete, the result will be divine.

Proficiency

A musician must be proficient with all the tools of the trade. It is essential to have mastery of technique along with a functional knowledge of an instrument's construction. Study and practice is a lifetime endeavor that illuminates the mind's way to approach anything representative as new. When you understand this, nothing will be able to create an impediment to your genius. Consider this. How would you act if you suddenly became enamored of a new form of music if you found it more to your liking? You must be able to internalize this as reality, without any fear or trepidation. Contemplate the reality of this possibility. It is an essential aspect of strategy.

Contingency

It is never sufficient to finish one section of a work, without having planned for continuation to higher levels of accomplishment. You should not become complacent with your progress and skill. If as a master woodworker you are going to construct a desk, you must plan for drawers, knobs, etc. If not, the work may appear to be esthetic; but, in reality, it may not be in harmony with the universe. Masters plan for contingency even if it appears that they are working strictly through an improvisational pattern. Presentation of an idea that appears to be an improvisation is only valid if there has been adequate study and prior preparation. A master "becomes the way" by being devoted to the art, and the art itself reveals its true identity to a master only when the "spirit of the thing itself" feels comfortable with the master as a vehicle for its own expression. The same applies to the craft and art of music. You must acknowledge and understand the source of creation and apply yourself with devotion, accordingly.

If you desire to learn my "way" of strategy, you must do sufficient research and study. Doing sufficient research means that you devote yourself as much as possible to the study of these ideas, to the degree with which you know you have accomplished what you want to accomplish. The level of commitment you give to "it" will indicate to "it" what to reveal of itself to you. In like manner, I knew what I was going to do when I began to teach via this book.

The Strategy of Mastering Two Things as One

In mortal combat it is essential to be equipped with more than one device should an inopportune situation develop. Warriors aware of this reality train to become proficient with more than their primary weapon, they understand the need to survive regardless of circumstance, to use everything at their disposal, and to act in accordance with that idea and belief. It is certainly the same for a musician who paints images from sound interpreted from a personal vision and who uses various "colors" to create a work of art.

A musician must think in those same terms to hear as well as recognize distinct expressions not generally encountered and, by overlooking certain elements, an impediment to artistic growth can ensue. In line with this thinking, a musician must also be able to perform in different genres from a perspective of knowing. Stubborn favoritism will always limit possibility and should not be confused with the virtuoso performance of a specific piece of music. A philosophic realty is that one thing does one thing, yet two things may do four. If you are in an entertainment modality, then being able to perform with various instruments will keep audience attention. It is hard to explain these ideas in detail because of their intuitive nature. Once you have understood the depth of the thing you are studying, the "spirit of the thing itself" will reveal itself to you.

Timing and Rhythm

Everything has its own time and rhythm. Though this would seem to be a simplistic reality, the fact is that most people and, unfortunately, many musicians see no reason to maintain a perspective of the right time and place for things, considering their own ego to be the predominant factor in the performance of their yet unperfected skills. This is a non-productive mentality: not understanding the requirements of what is required to accomplish mastery of the discipline they seek to master. As an abstract example, why would you want to play a waltz in 13/4 unless you understood the intricacies of 13/4 relative to a waltz translated into enjoyment for listeners and dancers? Unless, of course, you are just playing for yourself!

Nine Fundamental Strategic Precepts

There are nine fundamental precepts essential for the evolution and perfection of anyone wanting to accomplish anything of merit and long lasting worth. Know that practice and study are never completed. It is foolhardy to think in terms of having fulfilled all the requirements of study and no longer take into consideration the need for additional work and devotion. The "spirit of the thing itself" will do the same and the artist will suffer. When warriors think they have learned all there is to learn about their particular weaponry, they too will find that the spirit of the tools they use have also departed. If you will to devote yourself to a specific discipline, then that discipline must be the totality of your life. If it is not, then you are merely a pretender, and although you may retain proficiency on certain levels, you cannot consider yourself to be worthy of attention to be derived from a muse. Practice or perish!

The Precepts

1 – Always be sincere in your dealings with everyone and be aware of the need for the same with devotion to your art.

2 – The only way to ascend to greatness and to maintain it is with constant devotion and practice.

3 – Become familiar with every art you encounter. You will learn more about music when you examine the reality of other arts.

4 – Understand the "way" of other forms of expression to see more fully into your own without prejudice.

5 – Know the difference between right and wrong, with all people. Do not succumb to seemingly false advantage by lack of discipline.

6 – Strive for inner judgment and understanding of all things.

7 – See what cannot be seen.

8 – Overlook nothing, regardless of seeming meaninglessness.

9 – Do not waste time idling with inconsequential trivialities other than for simple relaxation.

Maintain an attitude of harmony with the universe to the best of your ability, and if your ability does not permit you to function as such, then demand of yourself *and* the universe that it does. These nine precepts will empower you to keep everything in your life in line with your personal quest for greatness to the extent you are willing to sacrifice. You alone are responsible for determining that.

Remember timing, rhythm, and the maintenance of harmony. You are not that special until you have decided that you are, based on your accomplishments, which will speak for themselves and preclude your need to become arrogant, conceited, and filled with false pride. Do not become jealous of others who may appear to be successful. They have also paid a dear price for their recognition that you cannot understand because you are you and not that person. You will always have a need to function in society, and it should be with the intent to maintain yourself in close proximity with the highest ideals you can comprehend through your own sense of self. Listen to your teachers. You have come together with them for a reason. There is no other way.

The old adage, played out perhaps, but still viable in the real world. How do you get to Carnegie Hall? Practice, practice, practice. When you have understood all there is to understand about your art form, continue to seek guidance, if not from a mortal persona, then certainly from the highest ideal of universal truth. There is no other "way."

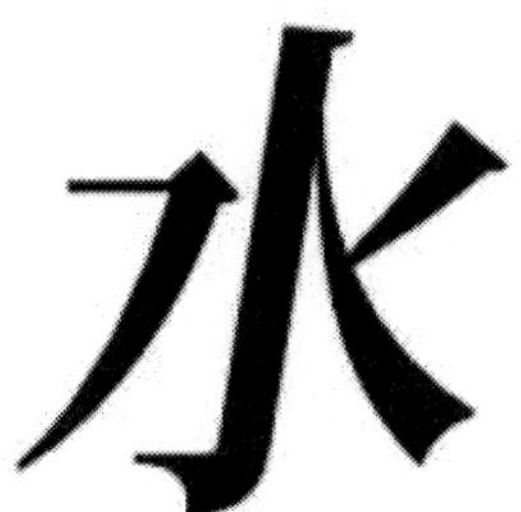

WATER

TWO
THE BOOK OF WATER
The Natural Flow of Things

In the *Book of Water*, I explain my entire strategy in depth. Things flow according to a pattern that allows all things, as part of it, to flourish as one. To force a result will eventually cause stress and will impede the beauty and joy of its expression. When water flows, it flows without restriction, and when it does encounter resistance, it determines a method for overcoming any obstacles in its path.

A seasoned warrior knows the required rhythm and timing for adequate performance of a deed and, in matters of life and death, it is essential that practice and constant study precede actual experience. There is, and will always be circumstances where one cannot act according to prescribed ideas about how things should occur. That is when the reality of having practiced comes into action and any particular condition be successfully dealt with to maintain excellence of performance. Having prepared yourself for, as many eventualities as you can think of will empower you to always forge ahead with intelligent and correct emotional response, not via a mode of panic and insecurity, but one of surety and confidence.

It is important to understand what you are reading in this book and to do so with understanding and retention. It does not matter that you can talk about my ideas to others, but rather that you can absorb these teachings into your heart and thereby overcome any limitation, self-imposed or not. It does not matter what others think of your performance as long as you know, without arrogance, conceit, or false pride, that you are putting everything into your work and not holding anything in abeyance in an attempt to seek favor from others. When you acknowledge yourself as the only reason for the universe to exist and for the universe to express itself in you, as you, and through you, you will express your music with true devotion to the highest ideal you can conceive of, and it will respond in kind. You must recognize yourself as the one and only greatest performer in the universe. It is only then that you can readily express this through the audience. This may seem a harsh approach to reality, but when you think about it, you will see that to do otherwise is to merely play at what you are doing. If you are going to play, play. Don't play!

Spiritual and Physical Bearing in Performance

A warrior must always maintain calmness of mind and poise of carriage. In this manner, personal bearing under any condition will always be dominant, especially when confronted with a matter that concerns success or failure. With a warrior in combat, it is life or death. With a musician in performance, it is ascension to an astonishing level or, at best, a mediocre performance. You may impress those who do not understand the matter at hand, but, for the erudite audience, mediocrity is always apparent and obvious and can lead to rejection of any further efforts on the part of the musician. This can allow derision to prevail and is the death knell for the artist who seeks to conquer all worlds, without considerable devotion to the muse.

Correct Stance in Preparation for Performance

In a ready position or a relaxed mode, a warrior is always ready for immediate action, should it be required. Likewise, a musician must not permit their self to slouch or to maintain a posture of improbability that limits communication with the instrument used for expression of a composer's offering. When approaching a difficult section or when learning a new piece, you should play as slowly as necessary until the arduous section is under the fingers via approbation into the heart. Physical stance and correctness of poise must be in concert with your endeavor. You have been taught to accomplish this by playing the particular phrase over and again, each time adding a bar before and a bar after until the entire piece is played at speed and without error in execution. As a warrior must have complete control of the sword, a musician must have complete control of the instrument. Only then will you express a performance with the highest level of certitude. The musician must handle the instrument in a manner that permits *its* soul to express through the hands and fingers and breath as it is the same for the person wielding a sword. Intent must always be sincere.

Contemplation of the Audience

It is wise to consider the audience that has gathered to hear your offering, the expression of which maintains the audience's level of expectation. A musician must always play from the heart, regardless of genre or intent. The audience will know what their ears tell them and if the work you are presenting has been prepared, conscientiously or not. If you present a shoddy performance, the audience will sense that and not express pleasure in the manner you would desire in the form of applause and acknowledgement. That is why genuine standing ovations are rare, and when given as cursory congratulations, is meaningless. You will know when you have given your all to your performance and expressed the intent of the composer, who may not have thought of the audience. You are responsible to the music, the audience and, finally, yourself to perform as if this was the very last time you would ever have the opportunity to perform for anyone, anywhere, including yourself.

Correct Breathing for Brilliant Performance

Correct breathing is essential for proper composure and calmness prior to initiating an expression of intent. Correct breathing allows the body and mind to relax and can help alleviate stress or tension that can interfere with your performance. Uneasy breathing will reflect through your body and instrument and dramatically affect the quality of your performance in the same manner that shortness of breath will seriously impede the most ardent attempts of a warrior in battle.

Properly Holding Your Instrument

Hold your instrument in a manner that indicates proper enthusiasm and reflects the joyous energy you put into the sounds and feeling you deliver. When you stand firm and strong your music will cause the same effect on the listener because of the level of mastery you are expressing through self-confidence; you will move in synchrony with the rhythm and emotion the piece inherently possesses.

Poise

Though mentioned above, poise cannot be overstated. It is the difference between a professional and self-assured manner in contrast to an attitude that could be disingenuous, or worse, can be considered amateurish. The musician's work is much more important than the musician until they are both one and it becomes evident to the audience. It should certainly reflect in your cognizance of what you are offering as an artist.

Correct Body Movement

Watching great conductors and great performers in the midst of their work gives an audience the thrill of being in the presence of greatness. The audience may not be aware of it, but they will certainly react intelligently and emotionally if they sense total commitment from the artist. Remember, music is not static—it moves. When a conductor is in the throes of ecstasy, when a performer is in the moment, it is obvious to everyone present. Watch great conductors as they exude a passion of certitude when they are conducting; watch great performers in rapturous ecstasy. With great dignity and aplomb, they cause the listener, in many instances, to reflect their own passion as they imagine themselves conducting the score as the music evolves and blossoms into profound sounds.

Different Methods to Approach a Performance

There are many ways to approach a situation, and each way provides a best action for the circumstance. One approach is head on, by intuitively knowing you will succeed in performance based on practice and understanding prior to playing.

Another direct approach is to examine all of the alternative nuances that must be uncovered before true understanding permits definitive performance, even after a thorough examination. If words accompany the music, what do the words convey? Where does the emphasis of the piece lay?

A third way is where you look at the piece through the eyes and ears of the composer and permit the emotions and intellect of the composer to guide you accordingly.

Improvisation

Regardless of the approach you take, you have to control the ideas that develop from the music. Jazz masters may play a piece repeatedly and, with each improvisation, they become more aware of the components of the music. The nature of improvisation is to understand the song itself; the approaches as mentioned will empower you to do that. If you are looking for patterns in pop music, look for the chord patterns that most songs have. In classical music, be aware of the changes in rhythm, time signature, tempi, etc. The result must always be the same—excellence of performance.

Understanding the Nature of Your Instrument

It is of significant importance to find the best tools for your craft. However, too much dwelling on trivialities can seriously impede the performance of anything, especially an emotion-driven art form on your chosen instrument. As you develop as an artist, the sincerity of your work becomes apparent, and you will be pleasantly surprised to find that the proper instrument for your level of performance suddenly appears as if out of nowhere, unless you motivate yourself to suffer the consequence of accepting that it will never appear.

Reality always rears its ugly head at the most inopportune time, and so it is the same with an instrument with which you are unfamiliar. Constantly changing models, keypads, and tensions of strings will cause unrest in the soul of the musician *and* the soul of the instrument. That is why many masters continue to play the instrument they have played for years, even though so-called new advances in technology have broadened the scope of the instruments themselves. Apparently, when dealing with a large instrument such as a concert grand piano, preparations made in advance will accommodate a visiting performer's exact needs. This only occurs, obviously, when the artist can demand such accommodation.

As a full-blown professional, realize that your audience will expect you to deliver an incredible performance regardless of what you are using to accomplish that.

Performance-No-Performance

There are times when you will naturally feel inclined to go over the top in performance in order to reinforce your own sense of self. It is at this time that you must detach from a need to impress anyone, including your own self. You will then find the work flowing at its own pace and without restriction in you and as you, with the joy and freedom required to become one with the work, without stress.

Becoming One with All Aspects of Intention

All aspects of intention suggest a complete awareness of everything surrounding the circumstance you define for yourself. Prior to directing your psyche to deliver a perfect performance, and your soul is calm, take into consideration all aspects of the performance, with yourself as the last. In this manner, you can readily overcome any form of fear because you have made the work more important than you are. When you have sincerely acknowledged your mastery, you will have no problem with this characteristic of being. You will simply be as natural as rain falling: exactly where you want to be.

No Preconceived Ideas

Never think of muses being on your side unless you have truly come to terms with acceptance of your magnificence, not with arrogance, but with certitude. At that time your consciousness will direct the muse to deliver according to your dictates, and by demanding with certitude, the "spirit of the thing itself" has no choice but to comply.

Playing Through the Audience

Depending on the level of performance requirement, you should have complete control over the environment to include the piece you will perform, the expectations of the audience, and the sincere self-aggrandizement of personal self-assurance. If you do not consider yourself the reason for the composer to have composed the piece, you will always seek to overcome a lack of perspective by trying to make it more or less than it actually is. This brings about confusion and the result is generally failure. Know who you are and where you are at all times. This takes practice, but once you accept your fullness of self, it responds with complete joy of its own expression and uses you as the tool of its expression.

Understanding the Composer's Intent

Though it is generally not possible to determine where the composer's head was at during inception of the work's creation, it is possible to grasp the meaning of the "notes," based on how they are placed on a page. Do they make an impressive "design," graphically? Is the title of the piece suggestive of something that you can relate to personally? Have you performed anything by this same composer, or have you heard another performance of the piece? Awareness of these matters gives you the impetus to interpret accordingly while you remain true to the "notes" you will create into music.

Combinations of Approach to Performance

When conflict arises between yourself, the work you will perform, and the anticipated response from the audience, the entire presentation can have a negative effect. To avoid this, pull out the stops in your personality and void their influence. Refuse to give nervousness any authority; do not succumb to the possibility of failure regardless of trepidation. Never perform half-heartedly, and, should an idea of failure enter your mind, turn it around in your head with a different attitude; your body and soul will follow suit. You will eventually be able to bring about any form of resolution without even thinking about it. This is the level of maturity of a seasoned professional, and you must demand of yourself to act in the manner appropriate to the circumstance.

All Your Heart and Soul

You must perform with intense focus, not the quaint notion of focus, but with internal demandment that your focus does not allow obstruction. When all parts of your being are in accordance with your intent, allow your body to carry your sensibilities into performance as a gesture of complete giving. Should you sense incompleteness, even during your actions, it is because you have not approached your task with conviction to overcome any possibility of failure prior to action.

Falling into the Audience

The audience exists only to accept your offering, and they will generally do so with no thought to your being incapable of delivering what they expect; nor are they aware of the madness and tears that accompanied your ascent to greatness. There will always be those who anticipate your failure, basing that on their inability to acknowledge anything higher than their own limited sense of self. They look to you as a performer to fail in accordance with their own weaknesses. It is essential that you understand this and that you adequately prepare to be able to confront any situation with your attitude of utter mastery, thereby annihilating any possibility of succumbing to frivolous ideas.

The Instrument as an Extension of the Body

Your instrument, your voice, your physical appearance—all must be in alignment with what you are doing. Do not overlook any of the three or you will fall short of perfection in your presentation as the paradigm of magnificence. The instrument of your expression must understand your desire as well as your technical mastery. Inanimate objects have a "soul," so keep in mind that the "spirit of the thing itself" includes all aspects of your giving and, thus, the instrument will respond according to your acceptance of its own mechanical grandeur.

Practice or Performance

Never differentiate between your practice and your professional performance. You cannot have a blasé approach to practice, even if it only consists of running over scales or passages countless times. The more you convince your body, mind, and spirit to perform as if it is the last performance you will ever give, be assured that when time comes for public appearance, your mind, body, and soul will be in complete accordance with your intent.

Bashful Butterflies

You must be utterly resolved to command the audience. You can only do this with self-confidence in the work you are performing and not the attitude of an immature child. A professional sees all aspects of what is to be delivered, and innately develops an attitude of dominance. The audience will notice that and possibly overlook any discrepancy in your deliverance. They will generally concur with your approach, even if it is something they are not familiar with; it all depends on how you approach the task.

Sticking to the Audience Like Glue

Though your primary focus is on the presentation of your performance, you must also be aware of the audience and the manner in which they are receiving and perceiving you. If something is amiss, you must recognize it, at that instant, dig deeper into yourself, and overcome any inadequacies you sense *they* are sensing. Not to do this is a primary reason for failure, regardless of discipline.

Tenacity of Intent in Performance

Regardless of what "piece" you are delivering, you must do it with the attitude of it never having been done to the level of your gift to the audience, and that you are establishing a standard for future reference for aspiring novitiates and other professionals.

Penetrating to the Core of the Listener

It is true of the target in combat as well as a person attending a performance that they are subtly prepared, perhaps, for you to overwhelm them by your approach and are in complete accord with being mastered and shown new realities. Do not permit your subjective self to identify with their inadequacies.

Being Tenacious in Your Self-Esteem

Once you have accepted yourself as the paradigm of performance virtue, you must never let up in your definition of what you expect the public to see and realize what you represent. This does not mean that you parade around exemplifying detrimental self-love. It means that you continue to develop your persona to exceed the expectations that you yourself will strive to attain without becoming lax in your endeavor.

Penetrating the Mind of the Listener

The listener awaits your penetration into their core; the listener is your target. What other reason would they choose to attend your performance and grace your presence? This is the attitude you must convey to your audience. If they attend in an attempt to denigrate your offering, then they are the ones with foolish mentalities. You must immediately ignore such possibilities and concentrate on delivering the best performance of your life for those with expectations of your grandeur.

Penetrating the Heart of the Listener

As you project your passion into your work and are sincere in your givingness, a sense of joy will convey itself to the soul of your audience expressed through their outward exultation and applause. Always aim for this level of performance, regardless of any personal bias of your own feelings. Accept responsibility for excellence in your art more than permitting annoyances to interfere with your performance.

Humiliating Debasers by Virtue of Performance

As you ascend to higher levels of perfection in your art, you are certain to encounter many others with less passion and resolve, people who only exist to criticize and attempt to denigrate someone who excels in self-esteem and self-enhancement. You must seriously endeavor to overcome any lack of personal fear and trepidation in your work. This is just as important as overcoming obstacles in order to learn what is considered an incredibly difficult challenge. However, with the attitude that you are in control of your own destiny, you will easily overcome these difficulties and, at the same time, emanate an aura of superiority when encountering people with hardly any self-esteem. If you succumb to the advice of others with so-called life instruction that they feel is to your benefit, demand that you do not permit any negative influence as you further define your self-determination and the ability to think for yourself.

Ignoring Diffusive Perceptions

In a personal endeavor to continue artistic growth and maturity, many ideas will present confusion in an effort to force you to challenge your own beliefs; this comes from life experiences. There is no escaping this, and it does not matter what extent you consider your own enlightenment to entail. You have had experiences in life that have driven you one "way" and then another. There is nothing wrong with these perceptions, as long as you maintain the desire to ascend to the higher levels of consciousness regarding your work and do not permit self-pity to interfere with any challenge you may need to face. You must damn the idea and alleged authority of self-castigation, at all costs. As you approach an understanding of my strategy, you will have to deal with many awkward conditions where you must reach deep within yourself to overcome any form of adversity.

Critics Will Always Continue to Come

Weak-minded people will always endeavor to bring down anyone with higher ideals than themselves. This is a natural state of the world, and you must be prepared to counter any objections to your vision. It is wise to be aware of other viewpoints and not permit them to interfere with your vision of personal magnificence. This is very significant, and if you do not understand these words, then reread them until you do. *You* are the center of the universe in your endeavors to attain greatness, and *you* must personally insist that nothing interfere with your ascension to higher plateaus.

Taking Advantage of Stage Presence

When you walk out on the stage, your appearance must project what you want the audience to expect. The adage about not being able to tell the book by its cover is a fallacy. How you present yourself prior to your performance is just as important as the performance itself in that you are addressing your own reality in the manner you want to be perceived as, with or without your instrument. Understand this! If you look less than glorious, your performance will follow suit. It does not matter what you may think of others in regards to their stage presence. Consider the success of those who not only have goods to deliver but also look the part of the correct deliverer. Think Liberace! Think Elton John! Think Horowitz! Think Dizzy Gillespie! Think what you perceive you will deliver. Think YOU! If you represent yourself in a slovenly manner or in a clownish mode, your performance, though most profound, will be considered on the level you have presented yourself.

One Chance to Win the Acclaim You Seek

It is only *you* and it is always *you*. When someone comes to listen to you and you have not prepared adequately for their expectations, then you have also not prepared for your own expectations. There may be times when a "second" chance may avail itself, but even so, there will always be consternation on the part of the listener *and* yourself to deliver what you presume to be able to attain. Never approach anything you do in life—even outside of your given art form and discipline—to be less than perfect, and do not pay attention to naysayers who attempt to deride you because of your dreams and their lack of accomplishment. If you want to be the master of your own reality, then you must accept yourself as that and overcome any alleged forms of self-denial. If you choose otherwise, then you may be a wonderful musician and draw accolades from your aunts and uncles, a very limited audience. You are either magnificent or you are not, and there is no in-between. Yes, it is all cut and dry. Refuse to be mediocre! It is all *you.*

Understanding Your Oneness with Your Overall Reality

There is oneness in the universe. Everything emanates from one source, and that source will deliver to you exactly what it is you want to experience and will assist you in overcoming any form of destructive tendency, should that be your desire. You make the decision to be that which you dream of being, never accepting no for an answer. I can go on and on with this truth, and I am sure, by this time, having read and studied my words to this point, you are getting the message. Should you still have difficulty in understanding any of my teachings, it is up to you to start again and demand of yourself to understand with retention what I am teaching you. Allow this mentality to guide you accordingly and you will be astonished at the results.

THREE
THE BOOK OF FIRE
The Passion Within

Passion and emotion are two separate things, and to confuse them will only cause needless concern as you further define your vision. Vision is your passion. Emotion guided or misguided by subjective thoughts and feelings will always interfere with the requirements of intended perfection, and the result of your work will be less than perfection. Passion allows you to overcome shortcomings in your hidden self-denial and catapults you to the heavens of your art.

The Passion of Your Soul

In pursuance of everyday activity, an individual's passion for life is evident in their every action. Focusing on the perfection of your ideal is a constant until you ascend to your highest level of achievement, where perfection must be maintained to prevent arrogance. When you arrive at the top of a mountain, continue to seek a higher peak. Passion insists that you know a work inside and out and that you are more intimate with the actuality of the music rather than merely the notes. To excel at anything, know it in your heart as real.

The Mental and Physical Place from Which You Execute

It is not always a simple matter of strategically placing yourself in the most advantageous position when preparing to perform. As an artist, you must take into consideration all the variables of the venue, where you are going to present your work. The physical position is most important, no question; however, should you find yourself in an uncomfortable situation for any reason, technically, physically, or otherwise, it is imperative that your focus for excellence is maintained. It is here that your passion must predominate through your attitude. Because your sensitivity as an artist is mostly subjective, you will at times possibly feel put upon without due cause and through no fault of your own. It is essential to maintain mental composure. Take all things in stride with a firm resolve, overcome any inconsistency, and perform without giving way to an emotional loss of control.

Controlling the Audience with Proper Demeanor

Demeanor is the poise with which you present yourself, allowing your passion to shine. The audience will sense this when your self-control is conveyed during the presentation of your work. Demeanor also encompasses your dress, your posture, your mannerisms, and your necessary self-confidence, without which you are merely plucking at string, notes, or pushing valves.

Variations of Control

First, control yourself. Having completely prepared for a performance is apparent when you have adequately come to understand the work. You will perform at a point where nothing will deter you from delivering a magnificent performance. Should you ever find yourself in a position of less than sublime repose; it is because you have not completely acknowledged yourself as the perfect extension of the work to be presented. Your passion in study will eventually guide you to attain a level of mastery that certainly goes beyond your own expectations. This is what you are striving for, as the practice you have put into acquiring excellence will become apparent in your self-assuredness, and it will be evident without you having to be conscious of it.

Second, control the performance. Visualize the performance prior to presentation to see yourself from a distance as the performer in performance. This is not a play on words, and you have no doubt, during your fantasies of magnificence sensed yourself to be outside looking in and taking exceptional pleasure in listening to the work you are performing. You have seen the faces of master musicians of any genre in an ecstatic state of bliss during their playing. This can only happen when you are the music and the music is you. Your passion for your work will drive this reality to the forefront, and your audience will know it.

Third, control the audience. The audience is there for one purpose—to express adulation without reservation for you and for the work you are presenting. It does not matter, and it should not matter where you are performing, or who they are. I cannot stress this enough! If you presume to perform for any other reason, you are in the wrong place and time. Control the audience with your passion to overwhelm them with grandeur, and grandeur can only be presented with the proper attitude of your greatness they must anticipate and recognize before you begin.

Suffocating Detractors

A musician, an artist, or a performer of merit and excellence will always encounter mean-spirited people, whose singular enjoyment of life is to see others fail. Such weak-minded mentality is mostly observable relative to the arts. It is essential that you, as an aspiring master, acknowledge them as irrelevant and with derision. Your passion, your commitment, and your life is all that should matter when on or off the stage. Smile and know they have no authority to impose their behavior on your existence.

Crossing into New Lands

Entering into a new area of endeavor can be frightening if you have not assumed mastery of your reality. The confidence you have developed throughout your training, practice, and study will hold you in good form if you have approached things in your world with dignity and aplomb. There is never a need to fear the unknown, and it is wise to recognize this newness with healthy respect for new possibilities. When you respect a new challenge, your inner self will maintain you and alleviate attempts by hidden insecurities to permit new challenges to develop an authority of controlling you, rather than submitting to your passionate approach and resolve to master it.

Understanding the Right Time to Do Things

With the exception of experimental practices, perhaps in closed circumstances, all things have their own timing and rhythm. It does not make sense to attempt a completely new technique in front of an audience that is expecting a straightforward performance. This is not the same as presenting a completely new form that you have worked out in detail, prior to presentation, and where the audience may have been apprised of something new. Remember the essential need to control the audience, the performance, and yourself.

Stepping on the Competition's Mind

You will always have competition in your desire to ascend to the heights of your own magnificence, once others who have like desires know it. It is at this time you must prevail with controlled passion to overcome any form of competition that can interfere with your ascension. You can only do this with utter resolve by not permitting any person or thing to stop you in your quest for greatness and magnificence. This is based on a passion for excellence that you must constantly nurture as an aspect of your being.

Collapsing the Competition's Spirit

When you acknowledge your accomplishments as without peer, and without permitting arrogance, conceit, or false pride to interfere with your higher attainment, you will know within that nothing can equal your level of perfection, excellence, or performance. Lesser competitors will readily recognize this in you and be intimidated. Always maintain an attitude of implacable stature, and you will have no problem in destroying the competition, doing so without overt gesture. A masterful attitude will prevail and overcome any attempt to denigrate your perfection.

Understand the Competition by Being the Competition

There will be times when you enter an arena that far surpasses your level of accomplishment. You may be in the presence of a greatness more developed than your own, and it is precisely at this time that you must assume the state of mind required to enter into the mind of the competition, without acting in an imitative manner. Seek to know at the immediate moment what is intimidating you, by looking deep within to empower yourself to use the competitor's strengths as your own. This takes time to develop and understand, but once you have done so, nothing can ever stand in your way to true greatness.

Releasing the Conflict of Competition

Conflict is a requirement for personal growth in every situation where you seek ascension to the highest levels of excellence. Understanding this will always keep you on the alert toward any potential interference. Develop the attitude that you are the one responsible for the intimidation of anyone seeking to usurp you. With sincere good intention, always project an aura of superiority without being obvious and arrogant. This self-assuredness can only be a result of your incessant practice and personal desire and endeavor to be the very best that ever was, is, or will be.

Pervasiveness

Pervasiveness is a constant projection of being master of the gift you have been given from whatever source of inspiration you acknowledge. It is a continuous seeking of the "spirit of the thing itself" to reveal more of its own perfection in, as, and through you. The responsibility of maintaining this level of consciousness at first may be overwhelming, but with serious consideration, it becomes a basic influence that continues to grow in strength and resolve.

Impressing Your Attitude on All in Attendance

Always believe and know the audience is yours to own. Even with strange nuances you find difficult to deal with at any particular time, your demeanor and presence of mind will overcome any sudden appearance of a challenge at the most inopportune time. It is imperative that you do not become obnoxious or overbearing in relation to the audience. They will sense this and immediately reject your most sincere and best efforts as imperfect and immature.

Scaring the Competition

In competitive situations, it is best to maintain the attitude that you are the competition for them and that they are merely pawns in your quest for ascension; they will sense this and become uncomfortable if you correctly project this attitude. Otherwise, you will find yourself in an awkward position of having to overcome needless gestures on anyone else's part. You must know and believe that you are the epitome of all you aspire to be and endeavor to accomplish. If you do not think in this manner, you will set yourself up for defeat, due to a lack of belief in your inordinate gifts that you have developed and nurtured due to diligent practice and resolve. Either you are the best, or you are not. There is no middle ground relative to magnificence and greatness.

Creating Unbalance in Any Form of Opposition

Devotion to your art must always be apparent to your psyche, in that you are constantly seeking to reinforce your skills and understanding toward what you are attempting to accomplish. The attitudes I am insistent upon are the very same attitudes that other masters and great geniuses before you have acknowledged and accepted into their very core. This is why when you see someone who has risen to the highest form of excellence and perfection; they will always have with them an unassuming air of mastery. That is how they got to where they are, and when asked about this sense of self they carry, subtly, but obviously, they will tell you the same. Believe this, as it is the only way. True masters do not hide wisdom from the sincere.

Overwhelming the Listener

The listener exists only to be enthralled by what captures their attention. You must never back away from increasing your influence, regardless of anyone's ability or lack thereof to perceive what you are presenting. You must perform to everyone in the audience, specifically, although you are performing for a collective whole. Realize that the only way this can be done is through total and complete commitment to performance and presentation, without consciously thinking of anyone in particular. Perform every piece with the attitude that this is the final performance of your life; the one for which you will be remembered.

Chipping Away at Uncompromising Demands

At times demands will be made by circumstances and situations that may appear to be completely out of your control. It is at this exact moment, as difficult as it may seem that you must demand more of yourself to take control of the environment. As a professional, you have to make decisions that will empower you to be catapulted to the highest level of performance. In situations where there is nothing to be done in the moment to change circumstance, you must proceed with all of your personal power and strength to take advantage of the situation, even if it seems implausible.

Confusing Detractors

Be uncompromising in your approach to the result you are seeking. If you waver in your stance, you will be targeted for ridicule, especially by those who are lesser than you are. It is the nature of detractors to find fault with every little thing they can identify. For this reason alone, endeavor to always maintain your perspective of excellence and ignore all forms of criticism, except that given by trusted teachers and coaches.

Three Shouts of Victory

Shouts of victory do not necessarily mean loud, verbal exclamations. The passion involved with your internal desire and external offerings are more to strengthen your resolve under any given circumstance.

At the outset of an action leading to accomplishment, the internal shout will give you added energy to fulfill your mission.

The second form is during the actual encounter where you further reinforce your resolve to bring about the result you desire to experience.

The third is the actual cry of victory that you and you alone, can share with yourself when you realize you have delivered the most profound performance you are capable of executing. The audience will recognize your inner bravado and react accordingly.

Moving and Crushing the Opposition's Body and Spirit

Should circumstances arise where you are caught in a web of sudden inappropriate action, determine instantly, without emotion, what is the cause of the delay or interference. If you sense derision from any aspect of a critic or possibly find yourself in a hostile environment, it is essential to overcome any lack of self-discipline that can cause you to falter. You do this by approaching the disturbance with an air of authority, not arrogance, or anger, but one that will empower you to overcome any resistance to your approach. Crushing the body and spirit of an annoyance is simply a matter of refusing to give it any authority in your life.

The Moon, Planets, and Stars

As allegory, the moon, planets, and stars represent the entire cosmos. Each is dependent on the other to function in harmony with the rest of the universe. Though chaos does make an appearance, at times, alleviation of confusion will empower success in the excellence of any endeavor. As a human being, you must understand the need for chaos and order to exist side by side to make a synchronous whole. To ignore one aspect in favor of another is a short cut to incompleteness because all aspects make the whole and not any individual set of thoughts you would wish to have dominance over any other. If anything is anything, then everything is everything. Ponder this!

Reaching into the Abyss of Being

You strive for perfection by acceptance of perfection. By denying perfection, seemingly overbearing obstacles will always be present. These obstacles are life demanding that you demand more of it for yourself. Learn to see obstacles as an impetus to demand more from yourself on a continual basis. When you find that you have reached the ultimate level of your abilities, you must demand of yourself to increase your capacity for additional enlightenment that comes of its own accord. Once you decide to further your accomplishments, reach deeper and, yet, even deeper into the depths of your soul and ascend to the highest level of reality that can be imagined and even more, so that the "spirit of the thing itself" will express itself in you, as you, and through you, based on your desire.

It Never Starts; It Never Stops

Every beginning has an end, and every end has a beginning. Once you attain a new freedom of mind, spirit, and soul, you will find that the end of that path is merely the beginning of the next path. There is no ultimate ascendancy to the height of accomplishment. Your complete devotion to the universal reality of your "gift," whether you have chosen it or it has chosen you, is never ending; revel in that truth and be glad for it. If not for its invincibility, you would have no need to exist once you mastered the basic rudiments of your art.

Know Your Area of Expertise

Every legitimate master constantly seeks to increase in understanding aspects of the universe as it relates to the work being done. True passion will lead you to this portal, once you have recognized your importance to the art you pursue. There will be many times when you will find yourself at the doorstep of a master of a discipline that is different from your own, and one that is rife with new perspectives you can employ for your own use. Understand the reality of this, as it is essential for you to come to terms with your own originality. Incorporating new ideas that may have previously been hidden from you, due to a lack of awareness, are a gift that comprises advances in your own personal self-edification. You may be surprised to learn that you now have a new set of skills to apply to what you are doing.

Releasing the Grip of the Unknown

As an artist, a musician is a person who continuously seeks higher forms of enlightenment to satisfy personal needs. At times, you may enter into an area that is fraught with possibly frightening conditions. Some of these things may actually cause you to run from them without considering your own needless fears. Be genuine in your approach to new things, with caution, but do not reject something out of hand because it is alien to you. Step back and look. If it is still more than you want to deal with, simply acknowledge it for what it is in your mind and leave it, so that you can always return to the possibility that it will function according to the needs of your desires. If you are sincere in your desire to ascend to greatness, the value it presumes may present itself again, and not having feared it out of hand, you may find that it is just what you need for your next level of being.

The Body and Spirit of Stone

These things I speak of with my own passion may appear to be harsh because they are direct and, in many instances, abrupt. Though I repeat myself over and again, it is to reinforce these ideas as mindsets that will empower you to ascend to the highest level of excellence and perfection. Because you have entered into the realm of universal strategy for the accomplishment of things that most people would shy away from, your approach and understanding of what you actually do endeavor to experience as your desire will manifest in perfect accord, but only when you have ascended to the level of acceptance that genius demands. Such is the passion of life.

Renewing, Always Renewing

There is never a cessation in life insisting on growth for its own sake. Life is an ongoing phenomenon that demands further definition of its own causality. It is the same for the musician who will ascend to the highest realms of the extraordinary. No matter how far you believe you have come, no matter how high you think you have ascended, you have not even approached the infinite that continues to beckon you into its embrace. The need for life to renew itself is evident in everything you acknowledge. You will never attain the highest level of mastery, because it is something that exists only in the "spirit of the thing itself" and the soul of the seeker. Never stop looking for it, and when you realize that you have made the decision to continue in your quest for the ultimate reality, you will find the ultimate reality welcomes you with all the joy and freedom that ever will exist. *Such* is passion.

FOUR
THE BOOK OF WIND
MEANINGLESS THINGS

As you travel through life with your discipline, fallacious ideas along with other unimportant entertainments not applicable to your endeavor will appear. Some will be obvious and others will be fraught with hidden devices to ensnare your mind into a belief that can be detrimental to your progress. Some will be firmly entrenched in the collective mind and be very difficult to release if you become entrapped. Some may very reliably lead to a bridge for you to cross, and you must be strong with your own presence of mind to either accept or reject what does or does not function for you according to your needs and your needs alone. There will always be someone to tell you what to do to attain a higher level of accomplishment and usually charge a fee. It is best to determine for yourself what is right for you, and though you may infuriate certain connections, you will still have the responsibility for your own decisions and not have to fall prey to the whims and wiles of others less than you are.

Schools That Teach Unorthodox Methodologies

Appearances at times becloud the reality of intent, regardless of presumed benefits, based on a marketing ploy to position the provider with a fabricated stance that can only detract a sincere participant by promising something that, in reality, is undeliverable. To impress this point, consider those who would suggest that the devotion normally required for mastery is something of the past, and with this new system, recently discovered, years of practice and focus can easily be ignored and bypassed. There are a great many among the populace that specifically seek out such bogus systems also based on their own naiveté that they believe will place them in the forefront of the dedicated and great. Be aware, that even though there are valid shortcuts that can be learned when well versed in a particular discipline; it takes much introspection and concerted effort to arrive at the point where it is, indeed, not a requirement to constantly refer to fundamentals. Mastery and perfection of anything simply does not work that way. You can twist and turn any idea to your advantage, yes, but in order to do that, you must know the rudiments intellectually, aurally, or intuitively. That is the way of music and art and only comes with dedication and practice of the sincerest desire to ascend to greatness. There are no shortcuts to perfection. Period!

Understanding Strength and Weakness in Other Methods

There are many who would propose to teach you something with "fluff rather than the stuff." In the mastery of music, as with any art, absurdities will abound that do take into account requirements that empower an aspiring person toward mastery. Be aware that these things do exist, but also be aware that once they are learned, it will still be a requirement to penetrate the depth of the learning in order to glean the most value that generally will still require study of the fundamentals. Again, there are no shortcuts to greatness. The longest road becomes shorter, step-by-step, and shorter, still, with devoted enthusiasm and acceptance of responsibility to overcome any limitations you have set in motion for yourself.

Long-Range Goals and Short-Range Goals

Recognize and understand the practicality of establishing long-range goals and short-range goals. Once you are aware of the differences in your agenda, redefine what you are attempting to master. Any aspect of excellence brings with it tried and true parameters that encourage further exploration of possibilities to enable a more functional ascension. While it is important to maintain a vision of greatness, it is also required that you do not permit your view to interfere with this vision. It is when the ego begins to assume authority over the true knowingness you are aware of; you will find yourself running into obstacle after obstacle. It is, therefore, necessary to maintain a perspective that ensures an ability to overcome any challenges encountered by going straight into the attack without wavering. This further empowers the use of challenges to attain superb overall beingness.

Coming to Terms with Odd Methods

No matter how much you may disdain clever methodologies, there will be times when you find certain things to your liking and will be sorely tempted to use them to enhance a hidden lack of self-assurance. This occurs for any reason, some you may not know exist in your subconscious. To say you should immediately deny authority to these compunctions would be fool hardy, if you do not recognize them in yourself, and this recognition generally comes from others in your life pointing them out. There is nothing wrong with this approach, and it a necessity for overall development to be able to come to terms with these anomalies. Once you are aware of them, they can be used to advantage; you develop personal style to empower the propagation of your art in you, as you, and through you. The "spirit of the thing itself" will always cover any shortcoming, once you are aware of an impending issue. This is accomplished by being very sincere in your desire and devotion to the development of yourself and your music.

How to Think of Speed and Endurance

Being able to finish a particular task in an appropriate manner that salutes you as well as you saluting the output is of extreme importance when striving for ultimate perfection in your discipline. A correct approach to your work based on concentration and personal demand is what will give you the added impetus to function with solid and lasting endurance. When you are tired and seek to find other means to get the work done, you will find that the work becomes more elusive and that you will have to force results that can never be synchronous with the higher ideal of the work itself. Rest when you are tired. This only makes sense if you are to continue in a quest for ascension. Do not fall into the trap of having to finish something in record time just for the edification of others who may be judging you. Proper function will naturally express required wisdom into understanding that in turn reveals itself as knowledge needed to empower adequate performance for the needs of all desires to attain fruition. There is no shame in recognizing the need to rest and regroup your thoughts and energies when you reach a level of tiredness.

Incorrect Attitudes

Foolish behavior is always the result of misunderstanding your intentions and those of a presumed audience. To take on the guise of something you are not will always cause strain and the need to use will power to maintain a balance. Will power must continually be reinforced to maintain its façade. Avoid it! Will, instead! Needless reinforcement drains the energy of accomplishment because it is misdirecting universal intent through a negative channel. To maintain correct focus and to avoid debilitating action, it is essential to endeavor to always be aware of your surroundings and the overall result you are seeking to attain. If you do not do this, you are courting disaster and diverting your attention from matters of relevance into matters of entertainment. It is never wise to be pompous, regardless of presumed certitude, even when you have attained the power and authority of your own inner self. Show business is valid, when backed up with authority to maintain a posture of superiority.

Focus and Fixation

Consider the difference between reality of devotion rather than obsession. To be focused means you are totally committed to your work and endeavor to control your personal development and growth. To be obsessed with something is to have no control over outcomes because you are subject to emotional whims at any given moment. Schools that demand you follow certain rules regardless of your own estimation are dangerously serious impediments to ascension. Forced to follow continuously changing rules will cause the "spirit of the thing itself" to constantly veer in its revelations and will cause additional confusion that will impede your development. Alternatively, focusing will permit direction and guidance of your intention in the most appropriate manner for the benefit of all concerned.

Foolish Behavior to Attract Attention

Braggadocio and aberrant behaviors may be entertaining to others and permit them to laugh at your gestures. The people who are usually in line with foolish behavior are mostly those who have no sense of esteemed accomplishment and they should be avoided; they are desperate for attention and will generally do whatever is required for them to be seen and applauded. But, whom are they being applauded by? Others seeking instant gratification and entertainment. Is this the direction you want your life to take? Is this the direction you want your work to represent? If it is, then you have significantly wasted your time in trying to understand my strategy of excellence and perfection.

Inner and Outer Attitudes

It does not matter what others may think about your approach to life and work. What does matter is your appreciation of the energy and commitment to your endeavor that you alone bring to bear. The tears, frustrations, frightening moments, and certain lack of sanity in all endeavors are what will mold you as the magnificent person to be. Your music reveals to the world exactly how you prepare to approach the world. All attitudes are relevant when it comes to performance and the proper balancing in your life relative to performance and everyday living; it is essential if you are to ascend to the highest form of deliverance. You do not comply with the ways of the world; you demand that the ways of the world comply with your demands. Nothing more need be said.

NO-THING

FIVE
THE BOOK OF NO-THING
No-thing, Not Nothing

My entire philosophy of strategy is summed up in this short book of no-thing.

You are the extension of all there is, ever was, or will be. Because you have the desire to ascend to the highest realm of reality within your given life time, the discipline you follow is a path for you alone, and it is not made for everyone. Everyone may enjoy music, but not everyone is a musician.

The universe is a filled emptiness, which is no-thing. A person will never have an understanding of this place inside or outside of the self until a genuine leap in consciousness is experienced. If you know something, you know something, and if you do not know something, it does not exist in your world. In the universe, no-thing is not a "thing" that is true and is not a "thing" that is not true.

When a person looks at something with subjective perception and does not understand what is seen, they say it is nothing. This is incorrect thinking. People, who study strategy and do not understand no-thing, do not understand their craft. All things are revealed as the desire for enlightenment is revealed by a person's own definitions.

If you would understand my strategy, you must be aware of as many arts but never veer from your chosen course. The accumulation of everyday practice causes the "spirit of the thing itself" to reveal true no-thing-ness to you. When you have truly understood the universe in relation to your music and your music in relation to the universe, you will have come to understand no-thing-ness. This is not a play on words and may appear to be a difficult concept to understand, but it is quite simple. Do not take anything for granted, and do not put emphasis on the "things" of other persons. In this way, understand my strategy. It is the *suchness* of everything.

No matter how intense and devoted your study, it is essential to become one with the art you pursue. If you do not become one with your art, you can never truly be one with the universe and the "spirit of the thing itself" will always elude you. You can play at studying for an eternity and nothing will emanate as excellence; things will never appear to be what they truly are. When you look at things without attachment, you will be at the place of oneness with understanding. The work is more important than the worker until they are both the same. When you come to see things in a broader perspective, taking no-thing as truth, you will see truth as no-thing.

There is virtue in the universe, and there is neither good nor evil. Wisdom exists, principles exist, and the Way of the warrior exists, but spirit is no-thing-ness. Let me repeat it again. The Way of the warrior is based on no-thing-ness. No-thing-ness is not to be understood as a "thing" because then it would be based on a conception of something, which would simply not be no-thing. The Zen term for "no-thing," which is the closest we can come to defining "no-thing," is called "mu." To understand "mu" means to understand no-thing. It is essential to be careful with intellectual definitions at this point. The issue is clear and I explain it as well as anyone else ever did or ever will. Regardless of literal translations or interpretations of my *Book of Five Rings*, you come close to understanding no-thing when you realize and accept that there is nothing outside of ourselves that can ever enable us to get better, stronger, richer, quicker, or smarter. Everything exists within. Seek no-thing and accept suchness.

If you understand what exists, you can understand what does not exist. This means that although it is impossible to know that which does not exist, we must take this to mean that if "anything is anything, then everything is everything." In the Way of the warrior, there is no such thing as thought, other than the intellectual powers you need to come to understand this terminology. That spirit is no-thing-ness means that there is no such thing as the self relying upon anything at all, other than the individual cosmic mind. This is the essence of music. It exists, and you merely grab onto it. It is the Creative Power of the Universe speaking directly to you, once you decide that it is speaking directly to you and to you alone.

I can go on and on forever in trying to explain the confusion that no-thing is or is not, but that would be exactly the wrong "way" to approach it. The Zen point of view suggests that you stop all conceptual thinking. Stop thinking about what you "feel" is right or wrong. Because all in the universe is simply no-thing-ness or "mu," there is no reason to pursue any attempt at perfection. Perfection is all there is, and when you come to realize this, you will have understood the "way" of the warrior, at which time you can forget about it and just be—simply be!

To KNOW IT,

IS ONE THING

To REALIZE IT,

IS SOMETHING

To BE IT,

IS NO—THING

YOU

ARE THE SPIRIT OF THE THING ITSELF

About the Author

Hanshi Stephen Kaufman has been in the martial arts for more than six decades. His rank and title of Hanshi, 10th Dan, is unsurpassed. He has written more than 40 books, including the world's best selling version of *Musashi's Book of Five Rings* and *Sun Tzu's Art of War*. Steve is extensively published and recognized as a major voice in his field.

His involvement with playing (tenor sax, soprano sax, and flute) encompasses stints, grinder gigs, and sit-ins with many notables, including Elvin Jones, Sam Rivers, Lynn Oliver, Bob January, and a host of others. He has studied with Joe Allard and Jimmy Guiffre. His computer compositions were created in the early 70's, when he taught himself programming by transcribing Charlie Parker tunes and solos via a Commodore 64. He has been playing, as he likes to say, "since music was invented."

Known primarily for his martial arts teachings and motivation methods, he contemplated doing this book, and when he mentioned it to music luminaries, including Jay Shanman: Newport Youth Band, Curtis Institute, Pittsburgh Symphony, Broadway; Dave Frank: Berklee Associate Professor of Piano, Dave Frank School of Jazz, and others. They knew it had to be "in the pocket."

Contact Steve at stevekayemusic@gmail.com.

Author Titles in Print

Ascensions to Greatness
Musashi's Book of Five Rings
Sun Tzu's Art of War
The Shogun Scrolls
The Sword in the Boardroom
Self-Revealization Acceptance
Practicing Self-Revealization Acceptance
Hanshi's Ultimate Guide to Self-Defense
Zen Stickfighting Self-Defense
Way of the Modern Warrior
Cherry Blossoms for Children
Lao Tzu's Living Tao
Napoleon Means Business
Lady of the Rings
If You're Gonna Play, Play
The Hanshi of Central Park
The Hanshi in Brussels
Portraits of the Living Tao
Homage for Miyamoto Musashi
Abracadaver and Other Satories
The Frozen Man

All titles available at www.hanshi.com/books
Email author at hanshibooks@gmail.com